MW01670618

Compulsive Hoarding

Understanding & Treating Compulsive Hoarding

Bowe Packer

TABLE OF CONTENTS

Publishers Notes

Legal Notice

This ebook is copyright protected. This is only for personal use. You cannot amend, distribute, sell, use, quote or paraphrase any part of the content within this ebook without the consent of the author or copyright owner.

Legal action will be pursued if this is breached.

Disclaimer

This publication is intended to provide helpful and informative material. It is not intended to diagnose, treat, cure, or prevent any health problem or condition, nor is intended to replace the advice of a physician.

No action should be taken solely on the contents of this book. Always consult your physician or qualified health-care professional on any matters regarding your health and before adopting any suggestions in this book or drawing inferences from it.

Bowe Packer

The author and publisher specifically disclaim all responsibility for any liability, loss or risk, personal or otherwise, which is incurred as a consequence, directly or indirectly, from the use or application of any contents of this book.

Any and all product names referenced within this book are the trademarks of their respective owners. None of these owners have sponsored, authorized, endorsed, or approved this book.

Always read all information provided by the manufacturers' product labels before using their products. The author and publisher are not responsible for claims made by manufacturers.

Paperback Edition 2014

Manufactured in the United States of America

DEDICATION

I dedicate this book to all those people out there who remind us of the things we have forgotten about ourselves.

And this holds especially true of my beautiful and amazing wife, Alma. She is the one woman who has the most amazing talent to let me grow and love the things about myself that I have not fully accepted.

I cherish the love she has for me when I may not know how to love myself.

May we all have this kind of beautiful soul in our life.

Sent from LOVE,

Sunshine In My Soul

PART I: WHAT IS COMPULSIVE HOARDING?

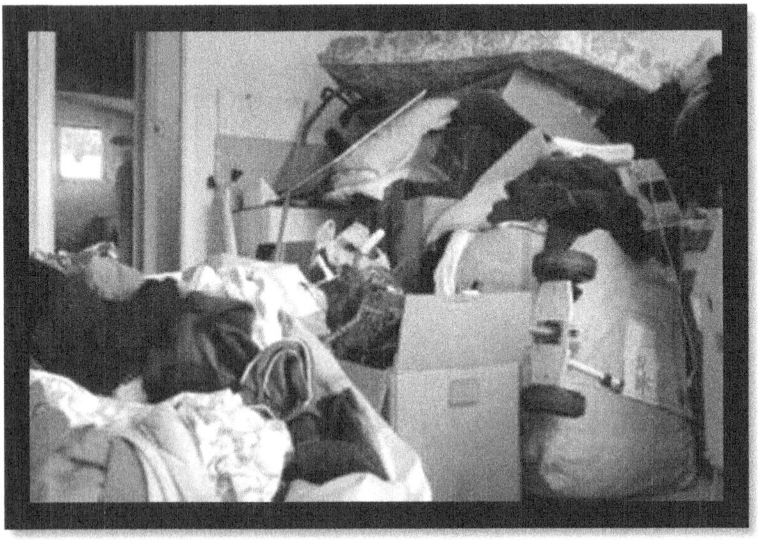

Compulsive hoarding has become a bigger and bigger problem through recent years. Approximately 3% of the United States population is believed to have this condition which may not seem like much but it's far larger than we would hope it to be. There's a reason for this, compulsive hoarding is a problem and it's very problematic for the people who are swept up by it and by those who are around them.

Now remember also that the 3% who are reported to have this disorder are only the ones who have come forward and admitted that they have a problem. Many do not come forward either because they don't see this as a problem or because they are too embarrassed to let anyone know their secret. So why should you care about hoarding?

CHAPTER 1-PROBLEMS ASSOCIATED WITH HOARDING

There are several different problems which come about as a result of hoarding. One is a danger to the individual who is actually participating in the hoarding behavior. They risk danger to themselves physically as well as mentally by participating in this. The mental danger comes from the fact that most hoarders are not capable of stopping the behavior on their own and require assistance to do so. They mentally believe the behavior to be ‘ok’ or even ‘normal’ and continue to participate in it despite what anyone may tell them.

This type of behavior can be dangerous physically because of the amount of belongings the hoarder possesses. Even items that are generally ‘safe’ such as papers or boxes can be dangerous in large quantities for a number of reasons. First, if the house were to catch on fire not only would the owner be unable to get out but their home would burn more quickly because of all the items inside.

Second, the fact that hoarding increases the amount of stuff in the home means that it can impact the structure of the home. Your house is only built to hold so much weight. For an average person this is no problem because you will never have enough stuff or people to encompass that much weight. For a hoarder however, it is entirely possible that the total weight of all of their belongings will come out to more than what their house can withstand. If this happens, it could cause structural damage could cause the house to collapse on itself.

The potential for fire is a big part of the reason that hoarding can be dangerous to the individuals around the one doing the hoarding. If the home were to catch fire the multitude of items within the home could cause the fire to grow too fast to be contained and could therefore result in far more damage to the surrounding area than a fire in an area not filled with so much stuff.

Now many people believe that the government or city or even just people in the hoarder's family should step in and take away all that junk. This will make them completely normal and it will solve the problem that hoarding presents. Except, unfortunately, this is not the case. If you take away all the belongings that a hoarder has managed to collect it will not get rid of the problem. It may actually make the problem worse.

The individual will simply begin hoarding again and will work harder to make sure that they do not get discovered by anyone. It will not take long for the individual to gather as much if not more than they originally had in their possession and no matter how many times that stuff is taken away from them they will continue to accumulate more and more. This process will never succeed without additional mental help for the hoarder.

Chapter 2-Where a Hoarder Lives

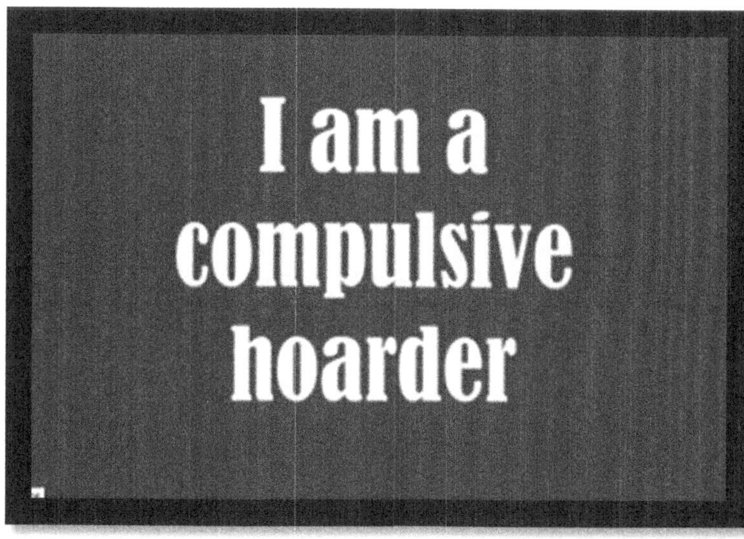

Now if you don't know anyone who is a hoarder and you're not a hoarder yourself then chances are you've never actually seen the type of home that a hoarder lives in. You probably have your own idea of what those homes look like but chances are your imagination isn't even close. A true hoarder's home is definitely something you have to experience in order to be able to believe it.

Bowe Packer

A few things that will help you to understand a little bit better:

1. The home is full of flammable materials such as newspapers, magazines, food containers, appliances, boxes and bottles.

2. Doorways and windows are blocked at least partially which can cause injuries as well as trouble escaping the home if there is an emergency of any kind including a fire.

3. Once the hoarder is unable to fill the floor space in their home any further they begin to purchase boxes that they can not only pack more things into but stack higher and higher as well. These boxes begin to be stacked on top of other boxes and other stuff and generally not in any type of organized pile. Many hoarders have been killed by their boxes falling on them so keep in mind this is a very real danger.

4. When too much stuff is piled on top of more stuff it can overwhelm the home. This causes floors to begin sagging under all the excess weight and this means that the walls begin to sag as well. They may also

crack or even collapse while second or third floors will often collapse without warning due to the increased weight.

5. Mobility is greatly compromised in these types of homes. Often there will be a small, narrow track leading through the home to the areas where the hoarder lives and moves. An average person or stranger coming into the home would not know how to maneuver through these paths and only the hoarder themselves will be able to manage it. This can become especially problematic when the hoarder is older.

6. Hoarders generally have trouble getting rid of anything which not only includes what the general public would refer to as useful things but also refers to things like food waste and even the containers those foods come in. These types of wastes often attract pests including cockroaches. A hoarder may even have a full infestation but won't even care.

7. Other problems may occur in a hoarder's home as well because they are unable to use their washing

machine or their stove because of the potential for danger. They also may have these areas covered in belongings as well.

8. If a room gets to be overfull with belongings and has no usable space anymore the hoarder may simply stop using the room and beginning compiling their belongings into a different room.

Chapter 3-What You Should Know About Hoarding Behavior

There is a big difference between being a collector and being a hoarder. Someone who likes to collect things can do so in an entirely normal way and not be a hoarder but there are three very specific traits to look for to determine if someone is actually a hoarder rather than a collector.

Compulsion

A hoarder doesn't have any choice about their collecting. They compulsively collect things either from shopping or from other people's garbage or road. These persons have an uncontrollable urge to keep gathering more and more and so they don't stop.

Living Space is Greatly Impacted

Because of the hoarding and collecting behavior the living space of the home is severely diminished. These belongings may have no real value but they impact the mobility of the individual living there. They are unable to move through the area or even use some of the rooms in their house.

Chapter 4-Functionally Impaired

The individual who is doing the hoarding may be unable to function in the home. They may develop a mental disorder such as depression.

If a person has all three of these symptoms then they are likely a compulsive hoarder. Remember that if the problem is actually a compulsion then that means the individual is incapable of stopping it. These individuals need to gather more and more stuff and also to keep all of that stuff forever. A hoarder may save things not just for a short time but for decades.

Think about it like this:

A woman who reached out to get help was having a lot of trouble. She had so much stuff in her home that she couldn't even get through it. She also had no family left because her children and husband had left the home when her hoarding got to be too much. The kitchen was full of food wastes and her living room was full of boxes of different things.

Her house is not even close to the fire department's code and if she doesn't get it there quickly the city has threatened to step in and do something about it. She's scared of what will happen but it doesn't take away the feeling she has, the feeling that she just has to keep gathering more and more things and that she can't get rid of any of them.

Whenever she looks at some new item she thinks about how it has the potential to make her life better. That magazine on the rack may hold the key to unlocking her problems. That table or broken necklace in the trash may be able to be fixed and therefore should be saved. Everything has the potential to be useful at some point in the future though she's not sure exactly how just yet.

The only way that she can overcome her problems is to seek out professional help. The first task she is given seems easy on the surface. Pick out a few things (just a few) that can be thrown away. When she picks out one she feels that it can easily be gotten rid of at first, until she actually places it into the trash can and begins to feel an extreme loss from that one small item.

CHAPTER 5-THE TRUTH OF THE MATTER

In order to truly understand hoarding and the hoarder themselves it is important to understand how they look at the world and how they think about that world as well. Chances are you have some misconceptions about hoarders and their behavior already. So the very first step is to find out what you have misconceptions about so that those can be remedied first. It's essential to look at those behaviors and understand why they are wrong and what the right beliefs are.

A hoarder is not, by nature, a dirty person. They do not like to live in depraved conditions or to have bugs or rodents in their home. They are not dirty people. They simply have a mental condition that does not allow them to get rid of anything. As a result, the individual may live in squalor or depraved conditions simply because there is nothing they can do about this side effect of their behavioral problem.

You should understand that hoarders do not keep things because they are too lazy to get rid of them. In fact, hoarders may expend a lot of time and energy to gathering new things or trying to organize the things that they have collected already. The difference between the hoarder and you is that the hoarder looks at the same world that you live in through different eyes. They see things differently than you do.

Imagine you walk by a dumpster and (just for arguments sake) you happen to glance inside. Your glance reveals that there is an unopened box of postcards. You may think that they look nice (based on the picture on the package) or you may simply shrug and walk on by. Chances are you won't do more than glance at the box. But someone with severe OCD that has evolved into hoarding will have an entirely different outlook on that box.

The person with OCD will not just *happen* to glance into the dumpster. They will look very avidly and they will definitely see the box. The fact that it's unopened means that this is a treasure and the contents of the box are extremely important now to the hoarder. They will take that box and when they get home they will likely feel excited about the contents and what they could do with them. They view this item as something to be treasured. But this feeling is something that they can't escape and that means they will continue to repeat the behavior again and again.

Now many people seem to think that someone who is hoarding is uncaring about others or that they are unaware of what their hoarding is doing to others. On the contrary, someone who hoards knows exactly how it can be. Most likely they are extremely aware of what it is doing to their family and how terrible it looks but they can't control themselves to stop. The behavior is stronger than they are and so they have to keep doing it over and over no matter what they *want* to do.

If the individual gets help then they may be able to overcome the problem. But they are going to need to want the help and they are going to need a professional in order to succeed at it.

CHAPTER 6-COMPILING AND COLLECTING

Step one is gathering all the items that are needed for the hoarder's collection. This could take a relatively short time or it could take a very long time. A true hoarder will continue to compile and collect for decades and will be unable to get rid of anything that may (in some fashion) be useful (at some point in time).

For the average person the things that a hoarder saves will seem unimportant or even garbage, but convincing a hoarder of this will be nearly impossible and will likely only result in further problems. They may insist even more strongly that the item is valuable for whatever reason and will likely condemn you for not seeing it that way.

If you were to tell the hoarder that you really wanted something that they had because you have the perfect use for it they would likely hand it right over because that's what they want, someone to find their items useful (after all they just knew it was going to come in handy one day). They wouldn't have any qualms about getting rid of the item if they believed it to be going where someone would appreciate it.

When people tell the hoarder that the items they have in their possession are junk or trash the hoarder tends to believe that the individual believes the same thing about them. They will begin to push that person away because no one wants to feel as if they are unimportant to someone.

Now for the person who hoards the act of getting rid of an item is like getting rid of a close friend or family member. It's like cutting off an arm or a leg. It seems irrational and simply impossible. The individual may want to do it but they simply don't know how or can't bring themselves to finally do it. There is a certain level of trauma involved in the throwing out process and the hoarder has an extremely difficult time with this.

Bowe Packer

Many people seem to think that hoarders are big spenders. They assume that a hoarder needs to have a lot of money to purchase all the things that they have compiled in their home. While this is true of some hoarders it is not at all true of most. Most hoarders are average individuals or even below average in the monetary department. They may not have a lot of money at all. But hoarders get a lot of their items for free either by gathering them from dumpsters or roadsides.

Compulsive hoarders see free stuff as presents. They believe that by 'rescuing' these things, they are keeping them out of dumps or landfills. They are saving the item for future use and they are also keeping our dumps cleaner, win-win right? Well that's what the hoarder thinks anyway.

You may look at a broken chair as being, well, broken. It's of no use anymore because no one can sit on it. If you're the crafty type then you may see it as salvageable and maybe if you're a woodcarver you may take it and fix it up. For most people however, it belongs in the trash. For a hoarder on the other hand that chair could be fixed up as good as new easily.

Now the hoarder may not know the first thing about fixing a chair but all they see is that the item can be fixed and they want to save it.

What happens when you get too much stuff for your home? Chances are you start getting rid of things right? Well that's the difference between you and a hoarder. For a hoarder there is no 'too much stuff.' They will continue to compile more and more no matter how cramped their living space gets. When they throw something away or they lose something it hits them as hard as the loss of a loved one would hit you. They attempt to do whatever they can to bring that item back home and save it.

CHAPTER 7-COLLECTIONS: FROM THE HOARDERS POINT OF VIEW

Chances are that you save things right? You save plastic containers to store your leftovers in or scraps of colored paper for scrapbooking. Chances are you keep these items neatly stored in one area of your home and in one small area of a room. This way they are available when you need them but they stay out of the way when you don't. If the scrap of paper is too small or the plastic container gets warped or stained you simply throw it out.

Well for a hoarder there is a difference. No matter how warped that container gets or how small that piece of paper gets it could be used for something. They are absolutely positive that at some point in time they are going to need that exact item and where would they be if they didn't hold onto it? Well they would have to go out and buy a new one wouldn't they? And all because they threw it away when they had it.

There are three reasons why a hoarder will continue to save something:

1. An Emotional Attachment-The hoarder may keep something that is emotionally special to them. Think about some of the things that are emotionally important to you. This may include pictures or a necklace from a loved one. Maybe you have an autographed baseball from a game you went to. These things are special to you and they have sentimental value. This is entirely normal and if you were to lose those things you would feel very bad about it. This is normal too.

   For a hoarder however, the difference is that the sentimental item because a piece of them. Losing it is like losing a limb and they can't comprehend what they will do without it. Where you may feel upset for some time, the hoarder will be unable to function. The item is a piece of themselves and without it there is no way they could move on with their life.

2. Usefulness-A hoarder may hold onto something because it has a use to it. Remember how we were talking about those plastic containers above? Well a hoarder will see those as having far more possibilities than you ever could and not just plastic containers either. Take-out containers, empty TV dinner trays and more could all have a use to them. For a hoarder it doesn't matter what they know how to do or what they are good at, if they found a box of sewing supplies and had never picked up a needle in their lives they would take that box home.

3. Physical Value-Finally, a hoarder may believe that an item is simply beautiful and should not be thrown away for that reason alone. They may decide that a broken wine glass looks nice sitting on the coffee table or that the multitude of figurines are too pretty to get rid of. These things are considered by the hoarder to

add a type of beauty to their surroundings and as a result, the hoarder couldn't possibly part with them even if they only add one nice spot in an otherwise horrid looking home.

CHAPTER 8-HOARDING ORGANIZATION

When you think about hoarders you probably think that there is no organization involved in the process at all. You think about the pictures that we painted above and assume there can be no method of organization at all and you would be right. A hoarder is by definitely a disorganized person. Because the compulsion has taken over their lives so much that they can't possibly do anything else.

Now think about when you bring something new home. You probably think for a while about where you're going to put it or what you're going to do with it. Imagine you bought a new lamp. Where is it going to go? You may spend time thinking about which room it will look best in or how you could place it to get the best light. Well for a hoarder none of that matters. None of it has a chance to matter because they simply have nowhere to put it that will affect either of those things. The important thing is that they have the lamp.

1. Randomness

   For someone who is not considered a hoarder the time to organize and declutter their home would be excellent. They would throw out many things that they've had lying around for far too long and would get everything else organized neatly so it's easy to find. Things would be cleaned so that when others came over they would be envious of how amazing the house looks.

   For a hoarder however, there is no compulsion to clean and organize. There is only the compulsion to collect more and more things. These things need to be stored somewhere and that means the new box of books could just as easily be stored on top of the pile of dirty clothes as anywhere else. The different materials don't matter and anything could be stacked in one pile.

   When you try and get rid of the belongings that a hoarder has you will cause them no end of anxiety. You look at a magazine from 1992 and think it's old. The hoarder looks at it and thinks that it's extremely important. You would throw it away, they can't bear the thought. Remember also that a single pile of magazines may in fact contain important things in their midst. A hoarder is not an organized person and that means there could be anything mixed into that pile that you would not see but a hoarder will insist on searching through everything in order to find any potential item of value.

For a hoarder, the idea of putting things away, out of sight (which seems normal to most people) is terrifying. What if they were to lose something? What if they couldn't find where it was? This is an awful feeling and it's one that most of us outgrow as children. If you've ever played peekaboo with an infant you know how this goes. When you're out of sight behind a blanket the infant assumes that you've actually gone away and they may cry. When you 'come back' they are excited and laugh. The same can be said of a hoarder whose items are hidden away in drawers. They assume that item is lost forever.

2. The Debate

   For a hoarder, the idea of getting rid of something is extremely difficult. They will think about each item carefully and very seriously. While you are trying to help them go through things they will endlessly debate and second-guess the idea of throwing out even the smallest of items (such as a scrap of paper).

In all aspects of life this hoarder will feel the same type of indecisiveness. They will continue to look through all the items again and again to try and find the right one or try to save the important things. When getting dressed in the morning they will have a hard time finding the right thing to wear. When eating breakfast they will have a hard time determining what the best option is. The hoarder will continue to debate and consider every item before they can get rid of anything and this causes the process to take longer and longer.

CHAPTER 9-UNDERSTANDING THE HOARDING

Hoarders may state that they are happy with their lives the way that they are. They may claim to enjoy the items they have accumulated and living amongst those possessions. In most cases however, this is not the case at all and most hoarders actually do not feel safe or happy in their piles of stuff. This is true for a great many reasons including:

1. Their family are disgusted or repulsed by the possessions or the home of the hoarder. Because the

hoarder doesn't want to get rid of any of their belongings they are involved in long and arduous arguments with family and friends. The structure of the family begins to dissolve which can lead to family members walking out on the hoarder and leaving them behind.

2. The hoarder knows what other people think of them and their belongings. They may be ashamed of themselves or embarrassed but don't know how to seek out assistance. They live in isolation and refuse to allow anyone entrance into their home. Children are unable to invite friends over as well and begin to follow the same type of defensive and isolated behavior.

3. There is always the threat of social services getting involved if the hoarder has children. If the home is declared unsafe or unfit then the child may be taken away and this is not something the hoarder wants (despite being unable to get rid of any of their belongings.

Chapter 10-The Different Types of Hoarding

Though we've discussed in general what hoarding is and how it works, it's now time to think about the specifics of hoarding and the ways that each specific type of hoarding actually works.

Common Hoarding

This is saving and acquiring common items. These are the individuals that keep clothes, old newspapers, lamps or papers. They will hold on to absolutely anything and everything that they can and will also collect free items from supermarkets, workplaces or even on the street. Anywhere they can get items that they feel have value they will and then they will keep collecting more and more.

Diogenes Syndrome

This is a form of selective hoarding where the hoarder saves things of low value. The individual often lives in extreme squalor and these types of hoarders do not care. They often prefer the squalor and hoard what anyone would consider to be trash. These items have little to no value even when compared to what would be found in a common hoarder's home. They may even store things like excrement for years.

Animal Hoarding

These individuals are extremely attached to their animals and may have hundreds of cats or dogs for example but they are unable to care for those animals. They continue to acquire more and more however no matter what happens with the old ones. There are three specific characteristics of these types of hoarders.

1. These hoarders always want more and more animals and don't have the resources or abilities to care for them all.

2. The hoarder doesn’t provide any form of care to the animals but does not want anyone else to step in and provide the care for them.

3. The hoarder does not see that the animals are suffering as a result of their inability to care for them.

CHAPTER 11-BELIEFS OF HOARDERS

Now hoarders are each very different. Just like an 'average' person, they each have their own beliefs and ideas but in general, they seem to share these common beliefs.

1. Physical belongings are as important as real people and should be treated as such.

2. Throwing away anything is traumatic, like cutting off your arm. It's extremely terrifying and it's better to simply continue accumulating clutter than to try and contemplate the issue at all.

3. The more physical possession you have the safer you are.

4. If an item is stored out of sight it might as well be completely gone. The hoarder will think of where items are based on the chaos in their home rather than the room of the house it should be in (couch in the living room, toilet paper in the bathroom, etc.).

When you forget something it probably annoys you. Little things annoy you less than when you forget something you've known for a long time and something you've always known will annoy you a lot if you forget it even for a moment. Well for a hoarder this is a little different because a hoarder does not want to forget anything at all.

If a hoarder reads something then they want to remember all of it. If they don't remember all of it then they feel like they've failed in some way. So they feel the compulsion to keep the article so they can be sure to have all the information when they need it (and they are certain they will need it). As a result they continue to compile more and more articles and magazines or books because someday they will need that information and since they can't remember all of it, they have to keep the actual article.

5. For the average person if you purchase something you want to take care of it until it's served its purpose and then it's okay to get rid of it. For a hoarder it's important to care for all of their belongings forever. This means you never get rid of anything. If a new pair of earrings came in a box then they must be kept in that box forever. That box can't be gotten rid of and the earrings can't either. If the earrings lose a stone then that stone has to be kept forever as well.

6. If you get rid of a hoarders belongings they will become irate and angry with you. No matter what item it is that you throw out you could even lose your friendship with that person because you are not allowed to touch any of their belongings.

7. There is a level of perfectionism to the hoarding process as well. In order to throw out anything the

hoarder must first know, absolutely, 100% know that the item has no further use and will never have a use. If they are giving away an item that does have a use they must know that it will have a better purpose wherever it is going. The item will also have to be perfect before it can be given away which means it will have to be fixed if broken and cleaned if dirty.

Part II: How to Help

Chapter 12-What to Watch For

Chances are pretty good that you're reading this book for a reason. It may be that you have a friend or family member who suffers from this disorder. If you know someone who sounds a lot like what we've discussed in the first section of this book then you definitely need this section. Hoarding tends to get worse as it continues unchecked so it's good that you're starting to intervene now rather than waiting. The circumstances will not get better without help.

We want to help the individual improve their living conditions through the course and use of this book. We will do that through assisting that individual in getting rid of their material possessions and getting rid of the compulsion to acquire and save those possessions but the primary goal is to assist the individual with their living conditions rather than the possessions.

Remember that every individual is unique and that means that no two hoarding situations will ever be the same. Remember also that individuals who are forced to get rid of things without the proper mental treatment will simply revert back to the hoarding behavior again and again. There is a full process involved in getting someone to stop hoarding completely.

No matter what type of hoarding the individual you know is engaging in it can be very dangerous and can pose extreme health risks both to their physical body and the health of that body. Being around so much stuff could result in problems such as colds or other viruses attacking the individual more frequently but it could also result in bodily harm from items falling on them.

Most hoarders will specifically tell you that they are not hoarders. They may even feel offended by your use of the word to describe their behavior. They will likely be able to tell you exactly what each item in their home could someday be used for and possibly even tell you multiple uses for each item. They've never had the opportunity to utilize the item in that way but it's there for the future when they do have the time.

Look at the list below and think about each item in comparison to the individual that you are hoping to help. Use this list to determine if the individual truly is a hoarder and if they are, we'll help you figure out how you can help them.

1. The individual is beginning to withdraw from others and refuses to allow others into their home. They have stopped allowing visitors for some time because of the state of their home, though they won't admit this to anyone. They believe that if no one notices the clutter then no one can force them to get rid of it. They may also use large curtains to assist in this blocking out process.

2. You find yourself talking to the individual constantly about their material possessions. You've grown concerned about the massive amount of stuff they have accumulated and volunteer to help them get rid of things, even as the problem first begins when the hoarder has relatively small amounts of stuff. As time

goes on however, you begin to notice that the hoard is getting larger and larger and start protesting more. The hoarder may tell you to 'butt out' and 'leave them alone.'

3. The individual is incapable of getting rid of anything. Material possessions are extremely important and need to be gotten rid of very carefully if at all. They should not be thrown out but should be sold or donated. Of course a hoarder generally does not want to take this initiative with their own belongings and don't feel like going through their own belongings because everything requires intense scrutiny before it can be disposed of at all.

4. The hoarder has continued to accumulate more and more whether through 'free' methods or through compulsive shopping. The hoarder will always have a reason for picking up the item and will have a use (or many uses) for that item that will take place in the future.

5. The hoarder will have completely closed off areas of their home that are too full of clutter to even live in or

function in. When their house gets too full they may expand to storing items in a garage, shed, storage unit or even their car.

6. The hoarder is indecisive about anything and everything in their lives and has trouble making any kind of decision. They will be unable to organize as well because there are too many different methods of organization that they could utilize and one must be chosen before anything can be done.

7. The hoarder is unable to function normally within their own home because of the multitude of belongings there.

CHAPTER 13-MAIN POINTS

Now remember that we're going to focus on the health of the hoarder themselves. We aren't focused on stopping the behavior. In order to stop the behavior it will be extremely important for you to get the individual help from a professional source and possibly from group therapy. You want to make sure you are getting the individual to a place that is going to be safe for them to live in. So try to help them get their home in a livable condition and then get them into some therapy.

POINT #1

A hoarder could put themselves at risk by accumulating too many belongings. Because of this, it is important that their house be made safe so that they can be physically secure while they are going through the rest of the intervention process. Everyone likes to have belongings after all. You like to have a few extra books lying around the house. Maybe you're a collector of comic books or art. These things are not necessary to your life but they are important to you and you would feel devastated if someone got rid of them after you've spent so long collecting them.

The same is true of a hoarder. They want to have belongings just like you and they've spent a long time collecting all of their items. It's taken them years in most cases and that means it's not easy for them to simply 'throw away' everything they've gathered up. They need to go through those things. But of course you don't want to sit around while they go through every single item in their home.

Point #2

You need to be sure you are approaching this situation as if it is entirely different from any other case of hoarding. Even if you have worked with 100 hoarders and helped them sort their lives back out you should approach this situation as if it is entirely new. That's because each hoarder is different from the next just like any other individual is different from the next.

You can read a lot about hoarding and you can find out a lot from this book and other sources but that's not going to tell you everything you'll need to know about dealing with your specific situation and the individuals involved in it. You need to focus on the individual who is doing the hoarding and not what the professional or even this book is telling you. Not every method will work for every person.

Take into consideration everything you know about this specific individual. You should know enough about their lives, their past and their friends to figure out the best way of helping them. You don't know what they need and what they want unless you talk to them so make that a priority. Maybe you can help them to reach some type of compromise.

Point #3

The hoarder should always be in the loop. If you're making any type of decision you need to let them know and you need to make sure that they are making some of the decisions too. The hoarder will feel lost without their belongings and they will likely want to fight you and keep much if not all of their belongings. This can be problematic but remember that there's little you can do without the agreement of the hoarder themselves.

Make sure that they understand you are doing this with them and not just for them. You are not going to take action without their permission. They are still in control. Having control will be essential because if they feel they have no control the hoarder may simply refuse to allow any help and will refuse to contribute any help either. This means that all of your hard work will go down the drain the second you turn your back on them.

POINT #4

Change takes time. You will need to help the individual to overcome the trouble they have had. Quitting a bad habit is not something that happens overnight after all. You're going to need to work with that person over a very long period of time. Even with the best of intentions and a perfectly cleaned home the hoarder is going to feel the compulsion to collect things that they see on the side of the road or in 'free' baskets. They will have to learn how to break the habit before they can ever be considered 'cured' of their mental disorder.

Remember that you are trying to undo what has likely been decade's worth of work. You are trying to break a habit they have spent many many years cultivating. It will take you a lot of hard work and a lot of patience in order to do that. It may seem like the individual is not changing anything but rest assured that they are doing their best and they are likely progressing at a very normal rate, no matter what you may think of it.

Point #5

Hoarding isn't always the biggest problem faced by a hoarder. They may have troubles with things like landlords threatening to evict them or social services threatening to take their children. These are the most pressing problems that you need to be willing to assist the hoarder with. As their support team remember that it's your job to help them feel as though they can overcome all of these problems and rise above.

Chapter 14-Tasks for Helping

In order to help the hoarder overcome the hoarding behavior you will need to focus on three separate tasks. These are:

1. Letting go of the past

   The hoarder must be able to let go of their belongings but those who are helping the hoarder must be able to let go as well. Why is it that you want to help this person get rid of their belongings? Were you embarrassed by their collection? Did you miss out on normal activities because of this hoarding? Many children want to help their parents get rid of their hoarding but feel neglected or bitter that they could never have a birthday party because of it or that they could never have a normal childhood.

   If you feel hurt by the hoarder then you need to let go of those things before you can hope to help them. If you don't let those things go you will actually be setting yourself up worse and you will be no help to the individual who needs you the most. You will also need to forget about what you think the other individual needs and focus instead on what they believe that they need. Try to find a balance rather than forcing your own thoughts and opinions on the hoarder.

2. Learning to understand

   You don't know that the individual is going through. You don't know what it's like for them to live in that home or get rid of their belongings. If you don't know then you could be setting yourself up for failure. You want to make sure you are thinking about the individual you are helping and not focusing on what you want or what you think they should have.

3. Be willing to forgive

   If you aren't ready to ask the hoarder for forgiveness then you aren't ready to assist them. They will need that level of understanding and you will need their forgiveness before you will be of any type of help to them. That's because you need to fully listen to them in order to help them overcome and if you don't forgive them for past wrongs then you simply won't be able to listen to them the way they need you to do so.

Part III: Preparing

Chapter 15-Getting Them To Accept Assistance

So now you're probably wondering how to get the hoarder to accept your assistance at all. If you lived with this person you know that they refuse to get rid of anything no matter what technique or method you choose. They believe that throwing things away will be disastrous and if you ever touch their belongings or throw things away without their permission it is a terrible offense.

Most likely you've tried everything you can think of to get them to relent and give up some of their belongings but you just don't know what to do anymore. You want to help them and you want to make sure they are safe, but they refuse to accept the help in any form because they are afraid you will throw away something that they need.

Chapter 16-Four Steps to Success

Step #1 Listening

You've likely always been told that listening skills are extremely important. Well if you're trying to help a hoarder then these skills will be even more important. You can't make the hoarder listen to you. Instead, you need to listen to them. Forcing them to do anything or trying to explain to them that they are wrong is going to be a lot like pushing a brick wall. You can expend all your strength and effort but unless you're The Hulk you're not going to get anywhere.

In order to truly listen you need to not just hear what the other person has to say but really comprehend and understand it. You need to think about the things they tell you and try to see these things from their point of view. You need to get rid of your preconceptions and your personal thoughts about the hoarding behavior and start to see things the way that they see them. You need to ignore that little voice inside of you that says they are being stubborn and listen to the reasons that the hoarder is incapable (incapable and not unwilling) of getting rid of the things they have.

Make sure the hoarder understands that you are truly listening this time so they are encouraged to continue. Use active listening skills such as paraphrasing the things they say, asking questions that are relevant to what they are saying and providing feedback that is actually helpful (not just something that you think will be helpful.

The most important of these is going to be paraphrasing. This is when you repeat what the other person said in a new way. You want to use this method not only to let them know you were listening but to make sure you understood what they said correctly. If you repeat back what you think they said then they have the opportunity to say 'yes that's right' or 'no what I meant was …' This way you'll be able to truly understand what they're saying without having to guess.

Paraphrasing can be an excellent tool because it tells the other person that you really were listening to them. In order to come even close to what they said you need to have heard them in the first place and in order to repeat it back you need to have been paying enough attention to remember it. This keeps the other person from tuning you out when it gets to be your turn to talk. It also helps them to refrain from getting too defensive. Remember the hoarder has been defending their actions for a long time. They want someone who finally understands them.

When you talk with the hoarder make sure you are not disregarding what they tell you. They are important too and they're thoughts and feelings are going to be the most important thing in this entire process. You need to make sure you are listening to those thoughts and feelings and also that you are providing feedback.

Feedback should relate to your opinion of what is being presented but remember that the goal is to get the individual to open up and not to get them on the defensive again. Present your opinions in a way that makes sense to the other person.

Explain that you are concerned they could get hurt or that you are worried they will become ill. These are things the hoarder can understand while explaining that they have too much stuff is something that they cannot. This is not going to inspire them to listen to you anymore.

Step #2 Be Sympathetic

Better than sympathetic, be empathetic. This means you feel bad for the other person and you relate to the way that they are feeling about a certain issue or situation. This can take many forms but it will be extremely important in this situation.

1. Ask open-ended questions that promote speech between you and the hoarder. Ask them about each of their possessions and why they are important. Ask the hoarder why they feel they should keep this item or what the item means to them. This helps them to see that you understand. It helps them to get rid of things as well because they know that you understand these items are important and want to understand more about it.

2. Don't ignore feelings. The feelings of the hoarder are just as important (if not more so) than your own. So think about and ask about the different feelings that the individual is experiencing throughout the process. If they seem angry then find out why, if they feel anxious then delve into that emotion as well. It can be extremely important to get feedback immediately so the individual does not completely shut down and refuse to do any more work.

3. Show that you are appreciative of cooperation. If they are agreeing to get rid of items or they are agreeing just to consider the possibility make sure you are thanking them for that and that you are acknowledging what they are allowing. These things take a lot of effort and they mean a lot to the individual, treat them like the treasure they are.

Step #3 Agreement

Finally you're going to need to find methods of agreement and negotiation. In order to accomplish any of your goals you and the hoarder are going to need to agree on what needs to be done and how it needs to be done. Chances are that this will result in some negotiations and several compromises. You're not going to agree with everything they think and they definitely aren't going to agree with everything you think.

In order to get started you need to find something common that you do both agree on. This way the hoarder will feel more in control of the situation (even though you agreed with them in this instance) and that will allow them to move further and to agree to more of your suggestions or ideas in the future.

Don't focus on the negative things that the hoarder says but instead try to help them feel more positive. If they make a negative comment about getting rid of their belongings then take a few moments to explain the positive results of the action. Explain the many things they will be able to do when the area is cleaned up rather than what they will have to go through in order to clean it. Remember not to antagonize this person because this will only result in further turmoil and trauma.

Step #4 Be a Partner

You are not telling the other person what they can and cannot do. Remember this. Instead, you are going to be a partner with them and you are going to help them to accomplish the task of cleaning out their home. Think about this, when was the last time someone told you in no uncertain terms what you were *going* to do? How did you feel about that? Even if you were a child and the person telling you was your parent you probably felt pretty annoyed right? Well the hoarder feels the same way.

This individual is the one that everything focuses on and they are the one that it should all be about. Put them at the center of the discussion and let them make many of the decisions. At least make sure they are in on the conversations and that they agree to any decisions you decide to implement. If you step in and try to be the boss you're only going to promote more and more problems and that's going to result in absolutely nothing getting done.

CHAPTER 17-THE CHECKLIST

Use this to help you discover what needs to be done first and what can be pushed back a little ways and dealt with later. You can print out this checklist for use throughout the course of your first run-through of the house. This can then be referenced as you finish different areas so you know what should be done and when it should be taken care of as well. For example areas with visible fire hazards should be taken care of before anything else and areas with excrement or urine should be pretty high up on the list as well. You don't want to leave these things lying around after all.

Checklist 1	**Place a check when risk/hazard is found**

Bowe Packer

Some areas in the home have visible fire hazards.	
Hoarding of excrement and/or urine	
Bathroom has no running water.	
Bathroom is unusable and unsanitary.	
Emergency personnel will be unable to enter the house quickly due to hoard.	

Windows cannot be opened from the inside.	
Doors cannot be opened or can barely be opened.	
Stairs are unsafe to use.	
Living room floor has clutter.	
Bedroom floor has clutter.	

Bowe Packer

Dining room floor has clutter.	
Materials are piled high from floor to ceiling.	
There are piles of heavy materials.	
There are unstable piles of materials that can shatter or break due to instability and weight (e.g. glass)	
There are sharp items mixed with the floor clutter or piles.	

Electrical wirings are unsafe.	
There are no smoke alarms.	
Smoke alarms are present but are defective.	
An area or several areas inside the home have pooled water.	
Structural damage is present.	

Bowe Packer

Stairways are physically damaged and are not usable.	
Rotting food is present.	
Insect infestation found.	
Rodent infestation found.	
Dead animals are found mixed with the clutter.	

There is presence of animal waste inside the house.	
There is presence of fluids such as blood and vomit.	
Some parts of the home are structurally compromised due to molds and other fungi.	
Running water is not present in other parts of the home.	

Electricity has been discontinued.	
Garbage collection has been discontinued.	

Next you want to find out what types of daily activities the individual is capable of carrying out in their home in its present condition. These can all be rated on the checklist below which can also be printed out for your use.

Checklist 2	**Rate the ability of the person to**

	conduct a specific activity **Scale: 1 – 5**
He/she is able to cook in the kitchen and prepare his own food properly.	
He/she is able to make full use of the refrigerator.	
He/she is able to safely use the stove or oven.	

Bowe Packer

He/she is able to use the kitchen sink and counters.	
The dining room table is not cluttered or is at least usable. The person is able to eat on the table.	
He/she can navigate the house safely and is able to access all the areas of the home.	
He/she is able to use the bathroom and the toilet.	

He/she is able to use the sink in the bathroom.	
When someone knocks on the door, he/she is able to respond quickly and he/she can reach the door quickly, as well.	
He/she sleeps in the bedroom and *on* the bed.	
He/she is able to do laundry (there is running water, washing machine is working, laundry area is accessible, etc.)	

Bowe Packer

He/she is capable of finding important documents with ease.	
He/she is able to care for animals adequately.	

PART IV: IMPLEMENTATION

Now you have all the tools you need to get started helping out the friend or family member who is suffering from this type of obsessive compulsive disorder. You know how to approach them and you know the different communication strategies you need to use. The last step is to actually put those tools you've gathered into practice so that you can get started actually helping that friend.

CHAPTER 18-THE SUPPORT TEAM

You're going to need a group of people who have this individuals best interests at heart in order to succeed. You'll need to make sure that everyone has the follow traits:

1. Patience and understanding
2. Resourcefulness
3. Problem-solving skills
4. Communication skills
5. Flexibility

Just anybody isn't going to be good at all of these things. You need to really think about your choices and you're going to need to make sure that each person you choose has at least a couple of these traits. If they have none of these traits they aren't going to be of any use to you and your goals because they won't be able to relate to the individual that you are attempting to help. Make sure you consider how the hoarder themselves feel about the person you are selecting to assist them as well. If they don't like the individual then it won't matter how great their traits are, they won't be any help to you.

CHAPTER 19-SHOULD YOU GET A PROFESSIONAL?

You may be considering getting a professional to assist your group. If you're looking over the lists we created earlier and thinking that actual repairs are necessary then you're going to want to hire a professional electrician or carpenter or whatever type of professional is necessary for those repairs. You want to be sure the home is structurally sound before you start moving too much. If the walls aren't supported well and are being held up by those boxes you will want to take care of that before you try moving anything.

You may need the assistance of a professional organizer if there is too much stuff for you and your small group (and the hoarder of course) to work on by yourselves. This will most likely be the case with anyone who has been hoarding for any length of time. Some of these professional organizers have even worked with hoarders in the past and may bring advanced traits into the situation which can drastically improve your chances of success.

Finally, you may feel that the hoarder is suffering from some other form of mental disorder such as depression and may need a healthcare professional in order to help them with these problems. In this case make sure you are getting them the professional help that they need. Some hoarders are found to need medications for depression or other illnesses and actually become more willing to help in clean-up efforts after they are given these types of medications.

Be wary of authority figures who seem to want to help. You may respect and appreciate their assistance but the hoarder may see them as interfering or even as wanting to get them kicked out. Try to keep government officials or the fire department even from being involved in the effort unless the hoarder is willing to allow it.

CHAPTER 20-THE PLAN

You will need to make sure you have a good plan in place before you get started. You need to remember also that your goal is to make the hoarder healthy and safe and that means focusing on them and their safety in the home and not getting rid of their belongings.

1. Work on health hazard areas first and try to get those areas safer. This could mean moving flammable items away from the stove or getting other items off of the stairs or away from fire exits.

2. Create a daily list of goals for each day which are small enough to be reasonably accomplished. Remember that no matter what the home looks like when you walk into it, the work is likely going to take more time than you even imagine that it will.

3. Monitor any areas of the house that could pose a direct safety threat for the individual. These could be perilous stacks of boxes or heavy items.

4. If you have an easy method of reducing the amount of accumulation then use it. Cancel magazine and paper delivery immediately. If the individual doesn't receive it then it's not their belongings and this will not be a problem to stop.

5. Get ahold of utility companies and make sure that bills are up to date and set to be paid automatically or through an online method. This allows the hoarder a

little less to worry about and ensures you won't need to go through all the clutter to find lost bills.

6. Try to locate important information like tax forms or birth certificates and put them away in a safe place such as a lock box.

7. Get repairs done quickly and properly by ensuring that a licensed professional is completing anything that is found to be necessary.

8. Help the hoarder to discover and create a routine that works for them and allows them to get rid of things when they are no longer needed and to keep only the things that are actually important such as bills.

Chapter 21-What to Keep In Mind

1. Get many boxes whether they are cardboard or plastic storage boxes.

2. Have a way of labeling all of your boxes either with markers or tape. This will help with the sorting process.

3. Designate certain boxes for keeping, giving away, donations, sale or recycling.

4. Use large garbage bags to hold trash and get rid of it as soon as it is full so the hoarder does not experience anxiety over getting rid of the items and try to get them back.

5. Use cabinets and folders to hold onto important documents and files.

6. Get a dumpster if there appears to be too much stuff to fit in a reasonable number of garbage bags.

7. Create a clear area to use as your base of operations.

Make sure you are speaking with the hoarder throughout the entire process. Without their assistance you won't be able to succeed and they won't ever maintain the efforts that you put into everything.

About The Author

Hello, my name is Bowe Chaim Packer and I like to see myself as an open, "***wear my heart out on my sleeve***" kind of guy.

Some of the most important things to me in my life are:

- Laughing
- Kissing
- Holding hands
- Being playful
- Smiling
- Talking deeply with others
- Being loved
- Loving others
- Changing the world one person at a time (if my presence in your life doesn't make a difference then why am I here?) Hmmmmm, maybe that is a topic for another book. ;-)
- Learning from others (although often times I first resist). However, don't give up on me....
- Sharing ideas (no matter what they might be)
- Learning about others via most forms of contact.
- Traveling – hello, of course – almost forgot one of my favorite pass times.

Bowe Packer

Remember, LIFE is a journey for each and every one of us. We must never forget the things that are important to us or lose sight of what makes us happy.

CPSIA information can be obtained at www.ICGtesting.com
Printed in the USA
BVOW10s0625020115

381596BV00004BA/4/P

9 781634 284110